AGING WELL
Living Long, Finishing Strong

JUNE HUNT

ROSE PUBLISHING/ASPIRE PRESS

Peabody, Massachusetts

ROSE PUBLISHING/ASPIRE PRESS

Aging Well: Living Long, Finishing Strong
Copyright © 2017 Hope For The Heart
Aspire Press is an imprint of Hendrickson Publishers Marketing,LLC.
P. O. Box 3473
Peabody, Massachusetts 01961-3473
www.aspirepress.com

Register your book at www.aspirepress.com/register
Get inspiration via email, sign up at www.aspirepress.com

The views and opinions expressed in this book are those of the
author(s) and do not necessarily express the views of Aspire Press, nor
is this book intended to be a substitute for mental health treatment or
professional counseling.

The information in this resource is intended as guidelines for
healthy living. Please consult qualified medical, legal, pastoral, and
psychological professionals regarding individual concerns.

For more information on Hope For The Heart, visit
www.hopefortheheart.org or call 1-800-488-HOPE (4673).

Printed in the United States of America
010817VP

CONTENTS

Definitions 9
What Is Aging? 9
What Is the Process of Aging? 13
What Is the Progression
of Adult Aging? 16
What Is God's Heart on Aging? 23

Characteristics 31
What Are Physical Characteristics
of Aging? 34
What Are Emotional Characteristics
of Aging? 38
What Are Mental Characteristics
of Aging? 41
What Are Spiritual Characteristics
of Aging? 44

Causes 49
What Losses Cause Discontent? 53
What Causes Contribute to an
Aversion to Aging? 54
What Is the Root Cause for
Agonizing over Aging? 59
What Ageless Hope Does God Offer? 62

Steps to Solution 68

My Personalized Plan 74

How to Overcome Loneliness 80

How to Walk in Wisdom 82

How Seniors Can Stay Secure
    from Scammers 86

Dear Friend,

I remember the day I began searching my heart for memorable role models—positive people who knew how to make the golden years golden. Suddenly, I realized I was already very actively involved with four extraordinary siblings—all senior citizens, who clearly knew how to live long and like it.

All grew up during the Great Depression, all experienced the painful loss of their father, who died in his 40s from tuberculosis. Yet each was exceptionally positive, especially in their senior years. They were the Ray family. Actually they were *my* family: my mother, Ruth—affectionately known by many as Granny Ruth—and three of her siblings, Swann, Pat, and James.

They were all encouragers, influencers, givers—all willing to help anyone, anywhere, anytime. Because their last name was *Ray*, I call them "Rays of Sunshine." (You will enjoy some of their wit and wisdom about aging scattered throughout these pages.)

Everyone seemed to smile when meeting Swann. And once they met her, they didn't forget her. In fact, people were fascinated by her—specifically because of her name! When she married Charles Lake, she legally became "Swann Lake," and she absolutely loved it! (Some folks surmised she only married Charles to get his last name!)

During her middle-aged years, she became an apartment manager, then after her husband's death, she established Swann Lake Realtors, which she managed throughout her 70s.

Even in her late 90s, spunky, white-haired Swann took great delight in making people laugh about growing older. With an endless arsenal of jokes and clever sayings about the perils of aging, she always began her short talks with a twinkle in her eye and a question on her lips.

How do you know you're getting old?

▶ You get winded playing cards.

▶ Your back goes out more than you do.

▶ You need glasses to find your glasses.

▶ Your knees buckle, but your belt won't.

▶ You sit in a rocking chair, and can't get it going.

▶ You sink your teeth into a steak, and they stay there.

While humor abounds about aging, consider these thought-provoking words: "Don't regret growing older, it's a privilege denied to many."

"Remember the days of old; consider the generations long past. Ask your father and he will

tell you, your elders, and they will explain to you" (Deuteronomy 32:7). I pray that God will use the biblical truths in these pages to bless you, give you hope, and encourage you to *finish strong*.

Yours in the Lord's hope,

June Hunt

AGING WELL
Living Long, Finishing Strong

Some people compare *aging* in life to an ordinary roll of toilet paper: "The closer you get to the end, the faster it goes!" This imagery makes people smile; however, for many, the thought of aging is dreaded like the plague. And, with today's emphasis on youth and vitality, the tendency is to believe: Old age is something everybody else reaches before we do.

Aging gracefully does not always come easily. In fact, one philosopher wrote, "To know how to grow old is the master work of wisdom and one of the most difficult chapters in the great art of living."[1]

**"Do not cast me away when I am old;
do not forsake me
when my strength is gone."
(Psalm 71:9)**

DEFINITIONS

What does it mean to *age gracefully*? For some, it means maintaining an eternally youthful appearance. To others, it means keeping pace with younger people.

But consider a different perspective that doesn't involve looking or acting any younger than our actual years. At the heart of aging gracefully is the word *grace*, meaning "a gift we don't deserve." God is a generous giver of grace. Therefore, we can experience aging *gracefully*, entrusting our lives into His care, leaning fully on His strength, and loving people with His love. In this way, we grow "more fully in grace" with each passing year. And in doing so, we grow more *faithfully* to the call of God in our lives.

> **"Your faith is growing more and more, and the love all of you have for one another is increasing."**
> **(2 Thessalonians 1:3)**

▶ **Aging** is a process of growing physically, mentally, emotionally, and spiritually in order to move toward *maturity*.

> *"Let perseverance finish its work so that you may be mature"* (James 1:4).

▶ **Maturity** in the New Testament is translated from the Greek word *teleios*, which means "complete" or "growth in mental and moral character."[2]

> *"But solid food is for the mature"* (Hebrews 5:14).

- God's purpose in the process of aging is to bring us to *spiritual maturity* by deepening our faith and developing our dependence on the Lord—on the presence of Christ within us.

- God's intention is that we *"become mature, attaining to the whole measure of the fullness of Christ"* (Ephesians 4:13).

Key Aging-Related Terminology

▶ **Gerontology** is "the study of old age and the process of becoming old."[3]

- The Bible presents growing old as an honorable and natural part of life.

- We may "live for the moment" when young, but with age comes an awareness of our own mortality. We take stock of our remaining resources (time, talents, treasures) and look for ways to invest them in people and projects that hold lasting meaning. Such was the case of Abraham, who lived to be 175 years old (Genesis 25:7).

"Then Abraham breathed his last and died at a good old age, an old man and full of years; and he was gathered to his people" (Genesis 25:8).

▶ **Life expectancy** is the average number of years of life remaining at a given age.

- Life span is the average number of years a healthy individual can expect to live from birth. Today people have an average life span of approximately 70 years worldwide.[4]

- Large variations exist in life expectancy from country to country due to differences in public health, medical care, climate, and diet. Japan has the highest life span in the low 80s versus Swaziland, where the life span is in the low 30s—less than half.[5]

▶ **Life expectancy** has increased significantly over the last 300 plus years:[6]

- In the premodern world, from 1770 to 1870, average life expectancy was only about 30 years.

By 1900, life expectancy began increasing in industrialized countries, but remained low elsewhere.

In 1950, the global average life expectancy was 48 years. This number increased to 60 by 1973.

- Today, an American man turning age 65 can expect to live until approximately age 84.[7]

And an American woman turning age 65 can expect to live until approximately age 86.

About one in four 65-year-old Americans will live past 90, and one in ten will live past 95.

Certainly as years are added to your life, your purpose continues.

**"The righteous will flourish
like a palm tree ...
They will still bear fruit in old age,
they will stay fresh and green."
(Psalm 92:12, 14)**

Have you ever noticed that while many people may want to live a long life, no one wants to "get old"? Because the age of 65 was designated as "retirement" age, many people consider this to be the first step into "old" age. Sometimes this has created a dread of reaching milestone birthdays. However, some things only improve with age.[8]

The Bible presents the seasons of change:

> **"There is a time for everything,**
> **and a season for every activity under**
> **the heavens: a time to be born**
> **and a time to die."**
> **(Ecclesiastes 3:1–2)**

▶ Aging Physically

- The physical process of aging begins from early fetal development and extends through our final breath.

  The Bible says our creation begins with God. *"For you created my inmost being; you knit me together in my mother's womb"* (Psalm 139:13).

- As our bodies age, we experience gradual change. How our bodies age depends, in part, on family genetics, patterns of aging, but also lifestyle choices. Fortunately, we can control our lifestyle choices.

The apostle Paul says, *"Do you not know that your bodies are temples of the Holy Spirit, who is in you, whom you have received from God? You are not your own; you were bought at a price. Therefore honor God with your bodies"* (1 Corinthians 6:19–20).

▶ Aging Mentally

- Knowledge gained through learning and observation becomes *wisdom* when applied appropriately.

"For the LORD gives wisdom; from his mouth come knowledge and understanding" (Proverbs 2:6).

- Growing older doesn't necessarily mean becoming mentally weaker. Giving your brain regular opportunities to "exercise" can help you strengthen mental acuity.[9] Therefore, you can set a goal to be a lifelong learner—and your brain will like it!

"I applied my mind to study and to explore by wisdom all that is done under the heavens" (Ecclesiastes 1:13).

▶ Aging Emotionally

- From infant to geriatric, handling and expressing emotions is an ongoing process.

"Hope deferred makes the heart sick, but a longing fulfilled is a tree of life" (Proverbs 13:12).

- Although aging may require slowing down for a different pace of life, this often presents opportunities to achieve emotional balance. Many seniors report feeling happier in their golden years.[10] This is especially true for those who place their trust in God.

"May the God of hope fill you with all joy and peace as you trust in him, so that you may overflow with hope by the power of the Holy Spirit" (Romans 15:13).

▶ Aging Spiritually

- Spiritual growth begins with learning about God and then advances to believing in Jesus Christ as your Lord and Savior and yielding control of your life to Him. This life-changing growth culminates in progressively becoming more and more like Him in character and conduct.

"I press on toward the goal to win the prize for which God has called me heavenward in Christ Jesus" (Philippians 3:14).

- By middle age, most adults have discovered that people, possessions, position, popularity, and power can't meet the needs of the soul. During this stage of adulthood we are often forced to come to terms with loss: the loss of a loved one, a job, health, or independence. We can choose to allow these losses to draw us closer to the Lord in a more intimate walk

15

with Him, or we can choose to go in the opposite direction, plunging headlong into a downward spiral of disbelief and rebellion against God. As we mature chronologically, growing in our relationship with Christ will help us mature spiritually.

Scripture encourages us with these words: *"Speaking the truth in love, we will grow to become in every respect the mature body of him who is the head, that is, Christ"* (Ephesians 4:15).

WHAT IS the Progression of Adult Aging?

Aging can sometimes feel like driving a car that is running out of gas. You press your foot down on the accelerator but the engine doesn't respond as expected.[11]

In God's perfect design, all living things—from plants to animals to humans—grow older and face aging. We all have a span of life, but some lives end at 3 months or 8 years or age 17. We are born, we grow, we play, we work, we live, we die.

> **"Show me, LORD, my life's end
> and the number of my days;
> let me know how fleeting my life is."
> (Psalm 39:4)**

THE SEASONS OF ADULTHOOD

▶ **Spring:** Early adulthood, 20–35 years old

▶ **Summer:** Middle adulthood, 36–55 years old

▶ **Autumn:** Mature adulthood, 56–79 years old

▶ **Winter:** Late adulthood, 80+ years old

This life cycle is marked and regulated by the change of seasons. Each season has its unique beauty in its time, each with a distinct God-given purpose of birth, growth, maturity, and wisdom. The Bible says that God *"has made everything beautiful in its time"* (Ecclesiastes 3:11).

SPRING

> "Our springtime years are lovely for the newness that they hold, for moments of discovery as passing days unfold."
> —Amanda Bradley

Springtime is *early/young adulthood*, ages 20 to 35.

▶ These are the years of seeking personal fulfillment, when health and energy are typically at their peak. The young adult years focus on gaining independence, growing in maturity, establishing a career, and for many, getting married and becoming parents.

"You who are young, be happy while you are young, and let your heart give you joy in the days of your youth" (Ecclesiastes 11:9).

▶ At this age, failure to grow spiritually results in:

- The inability to develop intimate relationships.

- Missing God-given opportunities in life by failing to follow a godly path.

"The seed that fell among thorns stands for those who hear, but as they go on their way they are choked by life's worries, riches and pleasures, and they do not mature" (Luke 8:14).

▶ During this season of life, an important measure of maturity is **trust**—recognizing and honoring God as our loving, trustworthy parent.

"Trust in the LORD with all your heart and lean not on your own understanding; in all your ways submit to him, and he will make your paths straight" (Proverbs 3:5–6).

SUMMER

"Our summer years are lovelier for all their sun and flowers, for the playful, carefree moments as daydreams fill the hours."

—Amanda Bradley

Summertime is *middle adulthood*, ages 36 to 55.

▶ These are the creative and productive years. Ideally, this season of life is spent investing time and effort in helping others and coming into a deeper knowledge of who you are and how your relationship with God can grow.

"When I was a child, I spoke like a child, I thought like a child, I reasoned like a child. When I became a man, I gave up childish ways" (1 Corinthians 13:11 ESV).

▶ At this age, failure to grow spiritually results in:

- Bondage to bad habits, burnout, hopelessness, self-doubt that leads to irrational thinking, impetuous purchases, irresponsible relationships, and midlife crises.[12]

- Untrustworthy character, lack of integrity, consistency, and purpose.

"Such a person is double-minded and unstable in all they do" (James 1:8).

▶ During this season, an important measure of maturity is **selflessness**—loving others sacrificially, guiding and mentoring them with godly values.

"Do nothing out of selfish ambition or vain conceit. Rather, in humility value others above yourselves" (Philippians 2:3).

AUTUMN

"Our autumn years are still lovelier for changes they bestow as we reap the golden harvest that the years of summer sow."
—Amanda Bradley

Autumn marks *mature adulthood* or the "golden years," ages 56 to 79.

▶ These are the years when physical decline becomes most noticeable, and leadership and control is often relinquished to others. However, with age comes wisdom, valuable insights, and understanding to pass along to children, grandchildren, and beyond. The golden years often afford opportunities for personal fulfillment, purposeful activities, and completion of goals.

"I was young and now I am old, yet I have never seen the righteous forsaken or their children begging bread. They are always generous and lend freely; their children will be a blessing" (Psalm 37:25–26).

▶ At this age, failure to grow spiritually results in:

- Rejection of others and self.

- A hardened heart toward God.

"They are darkened in their understanding and separated from the life of God because of the ignorance that is in them due to the hardening of their hearts" (Ephesians 4:18).

▶ During this season of life, an important measure of maturity is **acceptance**—understanding and trusting in God's wisdom and His will.

"I have learned to be content whatever the circumstances" (Philippians 4:11).

WINTER

"But our winter years are loveliest for the wisdom that they bring, and for the memories and friends that fill the heart with lasting spring."

—Amanda Bradley

Wintertime, or *late adulthood*, is the final season of life on earth, beginning at age 80.

▶ These are the years of dignity and self-respect, when we may require physical assistance from others, and yet think of ourselves as being in "the prime of life." And with God's help, we will remain doggedly determined to live long and finish strong.

"Never be lacking in zeal, but keep your spiritual fervor, serving the Lord" (Romans 12:11).

▶ At this age, failure to grow spiritually results in:

- Loss of meaning or purpose in life.

- Facing death without hope.

"So I hated life, because the work that is done under the sun was grievous to me. All of it is meaningless, a chasing after the wind" (Ecclesiastes 2:17).

▶ During this season of life, the most important measure of maturity is **wisdom**—seeing life from God's point of view, and therefore knowing what is true, right, just, and lasting.

"Is not wisdom found among the aged? Does not long life bring understanding?" (Job 12:12).

The God who made us also planned a wonderful future beyond the certainty of aging and the end of our days on earth. As Christians, we can look forward to that time with anticipation, while learning how to navigate the later years with dignity and grace.

**"As it is written:
'Eye has not seen, nor ear heard,
nor have entered into the heart of man
the things which God has prepared
for those who love Him.'"
(1 Corinthians 2:9 NKJV)**

God's purpose for aging is to provide us time for maturing—for growing up in Christ and becoming like Him in character and conduct. The longer we live, the more Christlike we are to become. Then, the more accurately we reflect Him to those around us, the more we will bring glory to God while still on this earth. The Lord's intention is this: The longer we live, the more vibrant our souls and spirits become.

The point is not that we are *aging*, but that we are *maturing*. This must be our focus. God created us for eternity. Ultimately, God is using our time here to prepare us for eternity there.

> **"He has planted eternity**
> **in the human heart."**
> **(Ecclesiastes 3:11 NLT)**

GOD'S HEART ON AGING

▶ **The Lord is your life**—choose to love Him, listen to Him, hold on to Him so that He will give you many years.

"I have set before you life and death, blessings and curses. Now choose life, so that you and your children may live and that you may love the LORD your God, listen to his voice, and hold fast to him. For the LORD is your life, and he will give you many years" (Deuteronomy 30:19–20).

▶ **The Lord's words are your life**—take them to heart and obey them so that you will live a long life.

"Take to heart all the words I have solemnly declared to you. ... They are not just idle words for you—they are your life. By them you will live long" (Deuteronomy 32:46–48).

▶ **The Lord wants you to love Him**—to acknowledge His name and call on Him so that He will rescue, protect, and answer you. He will deliver, honor, and satisfy you with long life.

"'Because he loves me,' says the LORD, 'I will rescue him; I will protect him, for he acknowledges my name. He will call on me, and I will answer him; I will be with him in trouble, I will deliver him and honor him. With long life I will satisfy him'" (Psalm 91:14–16).

GOD'S HEART ON MATURING

▶ **God's purpose for us is full maturity** by accepting Christ and biblical teaching from wise, Christian leaders.

"He is the one we proclaim, admonishing and teaching everyone with all wisdom, so that we may present everyone fully mature in Christ" (Colossians 1:28).

▶ **God wants us to become mature** by standing firm in the will of God.

"A servant of Christ Jesus … is always wrestling in prayer for you, that you may stand firm in all the will of God, mature and fully assured" (Colossians 4:12).

▶ **God makes us mature and complete** by testing our faith through trials.

"Consider it pure joy, my brothers and sisters, whenever you face trials of many kinds, because you know that the testing of your faith produces perseverance. Let perseverance finish its work so that you may be mature and complete, not lacking anything" (James 1:2–4).

The Long Life of Peter Roget[13]

If anyone had been keeping a weather log, the winter of 1779 could be ranked as one of London's most severe. In January of that year, a young pastor's family welcomes their newborn, Peter—a child who has likely impacted your life.

SPRINGTIME

Peter isn't your typical little boy. When he turns four, his father dies, leaving the home filled with heartache and hardship. His mother moves often, and his surroundings are depressing and dismal. Though Peter has a sharp intellect, he is anxious and restless, lonely and timid. History records that he lacks social skills and has few friends.

Yet young Peter has his ways of coping— unusual ways. By age 8, he is making copious lists of words. His natural curiosity and passion for knowledge compel him to bring order to things around him. He is happiest when he's collecting groups of words and organizing likenesses. Making word lists entertains him, but it's more than that. His mind coerces him to count things, including his steps, and forces him to be intolerant of anything unclean—a fanaticism that harasses him throughout his life. This little boy is unique, peculiar, and distinctive!

SUMMERTIME

These habits of childhood never wane—they are obstinate and demanding. His word lists grow longer through the tenacity of persistence. Peter has an uncanny grip on the associative power of language. He is proficient in linking thoughts and infusing phrases with clarity and precision. While Peter has no control over events that happen to him, he maintains control whenever and wherever he can. Had he lived in the present time, some might classify him obsessive-compulsive—perhaps even as one with high-functioning Asperger's syndrome, a neurological, behavioral development disorder.

Described by his mother as "awkwardly bashful," Peter becomes a medical student at age 14 and a physician at age 19— Dr. Peter Mark Roget. Limited, restricted, even handicapped by his social skills, he becomes less of a clinician and more of a researcher, directing his energies and endeavors to explore avenues that quench his diverse interests.

AUTUMN

He serves at Britain's National Academy of Science and as professor of physiology at the Royal Institution. He helps found the University of London and the Manchester Medical School. He invents the slide rule and the pocket chessboard. With his interest in optics, Dr. Roget makes significant contributions to film history with his research on the retina's capacity for "persistence of vision" and the illusion of motion. Improving the kaleidoscope becomes another one of his numerous passions.

He publishes written works on everything from tuberculosis to electricity, from nitrous oxide to galvanism, from animal physiology to electromagnetism and sanitation, and the list goes on.

He writes articles for the *Encyclopedia Britannica* and belongs to royal societies of physicians and geologists. He tutors and travels and converses with the likes of Benjamin Franklin's son and Erasmus Darwin, Charles's grandfather. Yet throughout adulthood, his love for the classification of concepts and cataloging of words continues with clear compulsion.

But along the way, he's dealt some hard blows. A maternal family history of psychological disorders is the backdrop of his life. When Dr. Roget is 39, his uncle (and only father figure) slashes his own throat in distress over his wife's death—he dies in Peter's arms. His mother's emotional instability surfaces as a young widow, and now her brother's suicide ushers her into acute paranoia. Roget's own wife dies of cancer just eight short years after they marry. Tragically, life for him is without humor and leaves him standoffish, distant, aloof.

WINTERTIME

Gifted physician, inventor, mathematician, scientist, and lecturer—Peter Roget retires at age 61. He lays aside his stethoscope and theories and picks up his word list again. Nothing he has endured will detour him from his love for words. All that he has accomplished in life contributes to his growing list of words. By the age of 69, his focus is solely dedicated to preparing his unique pastime for publication.

And so, at age 72, his list of "a thousand concepts" complete, *The Original Roget's Thesaurus of English Words and Phrases* is published in 1852—a work that has never been out of print. For another 17 years he continues to revise the thesaurus, making his last edits just one month before his peaceful death in 1869 at the ripe age of 90. His family continues his legacy for the next century, revising and adding to the word list.

Despite his lifelong accomplishments, Peter Roget's "retirement project" is what brings him notoriety. We owe a debt of gratitude to a list-keeping doctor for his *Roget's Thesaurus*—the sourcebook for writers, students, and anyone else in need of another word. The name "Roget" became synonymous with the word *synonym*—for generations to come!

By definition, "thesaurus" means treasure house. Consider: What will be the "treasure house" of your retirement years? Spiritually, your life can impact this generation and the next.

> "Even when I am old and gray,
> do not forsake me, my God, till I declare
> your power to the next generation,
> your mighty acts to all
> who are to come."
> **(Psalm 71:18)**

CHARACTERISTICS

Imagine having an older uncle—a caring uncle who would take kids swimming and fishing, crank out homemade ice cream, grow watermelons in his back lot, skate backward and stand on his head, polish common rocks in a tumbler, and learn to play the saw in his 80s!

Kindhearted encourager, my uncle James Ray was continually reelected County Clerk in Idabel, Oklahoma, for 30 years. He also agreed to be a "temporary" Boy Scout leader for only three months. Then, after 30 years of "temporary" service, his name became synonymous with scouting. He received the National Silver Beaver Award for exceptional character—the most prestigious award given by a council.

Prior to his death at age 87, *Camp James Ray* came into being, named after this humble, admired scout leader and man of faith, family, and many friends. Throughout his elder years, he continued to extend his hand of friendship to loved ones and strangers alike. And his life is a reflection of these words:

"A friend loves at all times."
(Proverbs 17:17)

Five Rays of Sunshine from James Ray

1. Experiment with new experiences.

One of the ways James Ray continued to stay young was the way he approached each new experience—with great passion and zeal—and sharing each new passion with others. He never swung a golf club until he turned 80, yet for the following seven years he could be found swinging golf clubs almost every week with friends. Though he knew he wasn't a great golfer, he immensely enjoyed playing with his friends and never stopped learning and trying something new!

"Let the wise listen and add to their learning, and let the discerning get guidance" (Proverbs 1:5).

2. Don't speak negatively about others.

James was fond of saying, "If you can't say something nice about someone, don't say anything at all." In fact, he lived that way himself—that was his reputation. No one ever heard him speak an unkind word about anyone.

"Let your conversation be always full of grace, seasoned with salt, so that you may know how to answer everyone" (Colossians 4:6).

3. Live by "The Golden Rule."

As his two sons grew and matured, not only did he encourage them to live by The Golden Rule, but he also became an example of giving and living a godly life. His legacy to them and others was this:

"Do to others as you would have them do to you" (Matthew 7:12).

4. Find a hobby—and include others.

James became a "rock hound," well known for his famous rock and mineral collection. He loved sharing this passion of collecting and learning about rocks, minerals, and gems with others, especially students. Always happy to take his rock collection to schools and share his knowledge with large numbers of kids, he was equally enthusiastic even when only one person asked to see his workshop and collection. He treated everyone the same, making each person feel special and important.

"Use whatever gift you have received to serve others, as faithful stewards of God's grace in its various forms" (1 Peter 4:10).

5. Look for the best and encourage others.

Believing in the "younger generation," he continually looked for opportunities to educate and encourage young people. As some people age, they become negative about youth, but he never allowed himself to fall into that trap. He looked for the best in others, always encouraging—whether young or old—that was part of his greatness.

"Therefore encourage one another and build each other up, just as in fact you are doing" (1 Thessalonians 5:11).

WHAT ARE Physical Characteristics of Aging?[14]

God designed our bodies to follow a normal flow of change as we travel through life and seek to accomplish the purposes He has for us at each milestone along the way. Just as we notice changes in vision, hearing, stamina, and strength, we will continue to notice numerous changes throughout our lifetime.

The good news is that God never intends for us to rely on our own abilities or strength—whether we are 22 or 102. His plan from the beginning has been that, at every age, we are to be totally dependent on Him—and Him alone.

During the latter half of our lives, noticeable physical changes will occur. Regardless of these changes, those who have a heart to spend time alone with God will make the most of the race before us. We can confidently choose to "finish the race" in the strength of God.

The apostle Paul said, *"My only aim is to finish the race and complete the task the Lord Jesus has given me—the task of testifying to the good news of God's grace"* (Acts 20:24).

Potential Physical Characteristics of Aging

- **Dwindling** strength and stamina

- **Different** sleep patterns

- **Diminishing** sight and/or hearing

- **Decreasing** appetite

- **Declining** sex drive

- **Depleting** hair pigment

People often say, "I've lived many years, but I don't *feel* old. Inside, I feel just the same as I did years ago!" In truth, we are not defined by our external body but by our internal character. God encourages us to rise above the limitations of our earthly body and persevere in becoming more Christlike in our thoughts, words, and deeds.

> **"Gray hair is a crown of splendor;**
> **it is attained in the way**
> **of righteousness."**
> **(Proverbs 16:31)**

Rays of Sunshine from Swann Lake

Consider this thought: Too many people worry about adding years to their life instead of adding life to their years. Well, my Aunt Swann definitely added life to her years—and to others. She would speak to senior citizen groups, sharing her unique perspective on "change" and its inevitable challenges. Her delightful talks on aging were always wrapped in humor and tied to clever anecdotes. She noted:

▶ Everything is farther away than it used to be. It's even twice as far to the corner and they have added a hill.

▶ I've given up running for the bus—it leaves earlier than it used to.

▶ It seems to me they're making the stairs steeper than in the old days. And have you noticed the smaller print they use in newspapers?

▶ There's no sense in asking anyone to read aloud anymore—everyone speaks so softly I can hardly hear them.

▶ The material in dresses is so skimpy now, especially around the hips and waist. And the sizes don't run the way they used to—the 12s and the 14s are so much smaller.

▶ Even people are changing. They are so much younger than they used to be when I was their age. On the other hand, people my own age are so much older than I am.

▶ I ran into an old classmate the other day and she has aged so much that she didn't recognize me.

▶ I got to thinking about the poor dear while combing my hair and I glanced at my own reflection. Really now, they don't even make good mirrors like they used to.

Isn't it wonderful when you find people who have the ability to laugh, especially at themselves. That's healthy. Laughter is like a good medicine.

"He will yet fill your mouth with laughter and your lips with shouts of joy." (Job 8:21)

Moving from season to season will bring marked changes in our lives. By God's design, the budding green of spring is gloriously transformed into the golden warmth of summer, followed by the varied hues of autumn, which then yield to the wonderful white of winter. Likewise, as the body ages physically, the spiritual life planted within will continuously bear beautiful blossoms. *"That person is like a tree planted by streams of water, which yields its fruit in season and whose leaf does not wither"* (Psalm 1:3).

Life is a series of choices, and it is our thoughts and emotions that directly influence our attitudes. When we deliberately choose to think positively, we create hopeful expectations for ourself, and our outlook reframes our life and creates greater peace when going through challenging times. But if we allow negative thoughts, anger, or hopelessness to take root in our minds and hearts, this state of mind can hinder our ability to have and maintain a positive attitude, and life feels burdensome and joyless.

"When times are good, be happy; but when times are bad, consider this: God has made the one as well as the other."
(Ecclesiastes 7:14)

Negative Emotion	Negative Attitude
Feeling unfulfilled	"I don't amount to anything."
Feeling unwanted	"I'm just in the way."
Feeling forgotten	"I'm a nobody."
Feeling useless	"I have no value."
Feeling fearful	"I'm afraid of the future."
Feeling discontent	"I'm just miserable."
Feeling helpless	"I can't do anything."
Feeling hopeless	"I have no reason to live."

Even when we experience losses in our lives, we don't have to live with negative feelings and attitudes. Optimism is always an option.

"Whatever is true, whatever is noble, whatever is right, whatever is pure, whatever is lovely, whatever is admirable— if anything is excellent or praiseworthy— think about such things." (Philippians 4:8)

POSITIVE EMOTION	POSITIVE ATTITUDE
Feeling fulfilled	"My life still has purpose."
Feeling wanted	"My life endears me to others."
Feeling remembered	"My life occupies God's thoughts."
Feeling useful	"My life has value to God and others."
Feeling unafraid	"My life is in God's hands."
Feeling content	"My life is filled with peace."
Feeling helpful	"My life impacts others."
Feeling hopeful	"My life is anchored in God's promises."

The best way to develop and maintain a positive emotional baseline is to mentally focus on the presence of God, the love of God, and the truth of God.

"May the Lord direct your hearts into God's love and Christ's perseverance." (2 Thessalonians 3:5)

Although we are limited in how we stave off the physical signs of aging, we have free will to direct our thoughts and emotions in a positive, godly direction. There are times when everyone—regardless of age—feels depleted, brokenhearted, and "ancient" in spirit, as Job laments …

"My spirit is broken, my days are cut short, the grave awaits me." (Job 17:1)

Because the mind rules the heart, as our thinking goes so goes our emotions and our decision making. As we age, some changes associated with mental processes naturally occur. Yet, you may be surprised at some of the positives that aging brings in these areas:

▶ **Sensation and Perception**

- Physical changes and impairments can lead to changes in mental acuity and perception (such as difficulty with mobility or lack of confidence when driving).

- Yet, older adults are often better at assessing a broad overview. While younger brains seem more focused on details to the exclusion of surroundings, the more mature brain can capture "the big picture."

"You will keep in perfect peace those whose minds are steadfast, because they trust in you" (Isaiah 26:3).

▶ Memory

- Some age-related decline is exhibited in short-term memory, while long-term memory shows less significant change with age.

- Yet, when older adults encounter a new experience, the brain makes a withdrawal from the memory bank to recognize and respond to similar circumstances from the past. This stockpile of experiences from the past enables older adults to adapt more readily to unique situations.

"I remember the days of long ago; I meditate on all your works and consider what your hands have done" (Psalm 143:5).

▶ Language

- Finding specific words may decline with age, but most language ability remains strong.

- Yet, if you are "always learning," studies show that you will continually add new words to your vocabulary.

"Instruct the wise and they will be wiser still; teach the righteous and they will add to their learning" (Proverbs 9:9).

▶ Thought

- More time may be needed to gather, store, and access information. Learning new information may be a slower process among aging adults who often need information repeated.

- Yet, the brain never stops growing. In fact, it continues to reshape itself in response to learning. Among those who learn to play musical instruments, researchers discover significant changes in the areas of the brain related to hearing, memory, and hand motion.

"Wise people treasure knowledge"
(Proverbs 10:14 NLT).

▶ Problem Solving

- The brain's two hemispheres specialize in different functions: The left side is more logical and the right side is more creative. While daily living and social activities for those over 65 are not typically impaired, it may take older adults longer to process information.

- Young people more often use only one side of the brain for a specific task. Older adults use both hemispheres of the brain at one time, thus using the full function of the mind to evaluate a problem or situation.

"I applied my mind to study and to explore by wisdom all that is done under the heavens" (Ecclesiastes 1:13).

Regardless of how we age mentally, our minds should always remain obedient to Christ. The Bible says …

**"We take captive every thought
to make it obedient to Christ."
(2 Corinthians 10:5)**

WHAT ARE Spiritual Characteristics of Aging?[16]

"It is not the years that make souls grow old, but having nothing to love, nothing to hope for."[17] God calls us to grow in spiritual maturity as we grow in years and life experience. How do you know when you have reached spiritual maturity? Those who embrace maturity reflect God's heart and Christlike character.

**"Therefore let us move beyond
the elementary teachings about Christ
and be taken forward to maturity."
(Hebrews 6:1)**

Mind-Set of the Spiritually Mature

Those who age gracefully will have …

▶ **Perspective on the aging process**

- Your life on earth is but a vapor. Consequently, the goal of every stage in life is to increasingly grow in the grace of God and in the knowledge of His Word, daily surrendering all areas of your life to Him.

- Your time is in His hands. You are content with His timetable for your life and the lives of your loved ones.

"A person's days are determined; you have decreed the number of his months and have set limits he cannot exceed" (Job 14:5).

▶ **Courage to accept change**

- Christ is the greatest change agent. He changes you from being immature to being a mature Christian who trusts Him for every challenge.

- Change is a fact of life. Christ gives you confidence to make the needed changes to become more like Him.

"I eagerly expect and hope that I will in no way be ashamed, but will have sufficient courage so that now as always Christ will be exalted in my body, whether by life or by death" (Philippians 1:20).

▶ Commitment to godly values

- Loving God means embracing His values as your own and making decisions that line up with His instructions regarding how you are to live.

- Life is a series of choices, choosing right over wrong because of a desire to please Him.

"Who, then, are those who fear the LORD? He will instruct them in the ways they should choose" (Psalm 25:12).

▶ Acceptance of yourself and others

- Acknowledge that you have been accepted by God, the foundation on which your relationship grows more precious through the years.

- Acceptance of others flows from acceptance of yourself as being acceptable to Christ.

"Accept one another, then, just as Christ accepted you, in order to bring praise to God" (Romans 15:7).

▶ Ability to laugh at your weaknesses

- Learning the truth about your weaknesses allows you to rest in God's provision without trying to work for His approval.

- Life is short and God forgives, so you can laugh at your mistakes and weaknesses.

"A cheerful heart is good medicine"
(Proverbs 17:22).

▶ Humility to admit your mistakes

- God's sacrificial love—expressed in Jesus' humbling Himself, becoming a man, and dying on the cross for you when you were dead in your sins and estranged from Him— demands that you be humble.

- God will lead and teach you if you are mature enough to admit your mistakes and learn from them.

"He guides the humble in what is right and teaches them his way" (Psalm 25:9).

▶ Desire to serve others

- Just as Jesus came to serve rather than be served, you should serve by praying, encouraging, and training others how to study and apply God's Word.

- Ask, "What can I do that is most loving for others?"

"Jesus … said, 'Anyone who wants to be first must be the very last, and the servant of all' " (Mark 9:35).

▶ Ability to live one day at a time

- Since you have no guarantee of tomorrow, each day is to be lived fully depending on God, listening for His direction, seeking His will so that you will honor Him in all you do.

- Say, "I will thank God for something each day."

"This is the day the LORD has made; we will rejoice and be glad in it" (Psalm 118:24 NKJV).

▶ Deepening of faith and hope for the future

- Learning God's Word and applying His truth allows God to operate in your life in ways that prove His trustworthiness and increase your faith in the future He has planned for you.

- Let the truth of Isaiah 46:4 give hope for your heart.

"Even to your old age and gray hairs I am he, I am he who will sustain you. I have made you and I will carry you; I will sustain you and I will rescue you" (Isaiah 46:4).

CAUSES

Living in the small town of Idabel, Oklahoma, my uncle Pat Ray was only 15 years old when his father died. As the oldest of two children, he and his sister Swann dropped out of high school to find jobs—motivated by their desire to help their mother provide for the family.

A few years later, Pat moved to Ada, Oklahoma, where he sold insurance and then owned a car dealership. His priority was always helping people—either to get on their feet or to get out of trouble.

Their youngest brother, Billy, was the black sheep of the family—an alcoholic who lost his wife, his health, and his business. (Billy's business partner ran off with Billy's money—and his wife.) Sadly, Billy died by suicide. Not only did he leave this world through painful circumstances, but also with great indebtedness.

Ever honorable, Pat felt duty bound to see that Billy's debtors would be paid. So Pat moved to Shreveport for two years to work at Billy's refrigerator/freezer business. His goal was to pay his brother's debts in full. Despite being under no business obligation to do this, Pat simply believed it was the *right* thing to do.

Indeed, like Jesus, he paid a debt he did not owe. Pat lived out this verse ...

"Let no debt remain outstanding, except the continuing debt to love one another, for whoever loves others has fulfilled the law."
(Romans 13:8)

Rays of Sunshine from Pat Ray—Age 84

Five Daily Don'ts When Aging

1. Don't live with self-pity about losses.

"There's no room for self-pity—there are so many things we can still enjoy. So let's enjoy life now, because one day this life will come to a close. Today we can see value in what, yesterday, we were too busy to see."

"Everyone has losses (I've lost two wives), but I need to thank God for the people who are in my life now. I need to thank God specifically for what I can enjoy today: the beauty outdoors, phoning my friends, playing games, or helping my neighbor. I love to help people—God just made me that way."

"Instead of focusing on what we *don't have*, we need to thank God for what we *do have*."

First Thessalonians 5:18 says, *"Give thanks in all circumstances; for this is God's will for you in Christ Jesus."*

2. Don't live with pessimism about the future.

"There's also no room for pessimism if we fill our hearts with hope. There is no room to be pessimistic about the future! Instead, there's room in each heart for hope—hope that people will know they are loved and valued, hope of having peace in their hearts no matter the circumstances."

Romans 15:13 says, *"May the God of hope fill you with all joy and peace as you trust in him, so that you may overflow with hope by the power of the Holy Spirit."*

3. Don't live to win an argument.

"I learned all about arguing when I was a little boy. My folks let me go downtown on Saturday, and I would go for one purpose: to see two, tall, old men who knew the Bible verbatim. These elderly men had memorized about every verse in the Bible and came downtown *not to discuss* the Bible reasonably, but *to argue* about the Bible—contentiously. And of course, the more they argued the further apart they got. So I learned then and there, don't argue. There is no such thing as winning an argument by arguing."

First Peter 3:15 says, *"Always be prepared to give an answer to everyone who asks you to give the reason for the hope that you have. But do this with gentleness and respect."*

4. Don't live isolated from family and friends.

"When asked, 'Don't you get lonely?' I say, 'No, I have a phone. I have a hand. I can pick up the phone and call a friend.' So, let's get out in the world. See old friends. Don't lose contact with family and friends. Life is a lot different now because of my age, but it's just as full. There's a lot of pleasure in giving and I want to share that happiness and God's love with as many people as I can."

Acts 20:35 says, *"We must help the weak, remembering the words the Lord Jesus himself said: 'It is more blessed to give than to receive.'"*

5. Don't live with doubts about God's direction.

"At times I felt I was slower in accomplishing my goals than I wanted. But looking back, I can honestly say I usually got there. I never felt I was smart enough to doubt God."

Psalm 32:8 says, *"I will instruct you and teach you in the way you should go; I will counsel you with my loving eye on you."*

Consider the common peach tree: In its first year, the top growth of a peach tree is *pruned back* 50% in order to receive better access to light and air movement. This loss is necessary for growth. As God grows you, He also allows loss. You will not mature as He intends if you have an imbalanced focus on what "once was." Yet, if you entrust your losses to the Lord and focus on the future He has planned, you won't be embittered in your later years.

Growth of any kind involves many forms of loss, and aging *means more loss*. If we live in the past, longing for what "once was," there is no spiritual growth and little chance of finding joy in *today*. Maturity fails to take root in the infertile soil of prolonged grief and depression, but discontent is quick to flourish there.

Losses Leading to Discontentment

- Loss of control
- Loss of health
- Loss of home
- Loss of dreams
- Loss of purpose
- Loss of hope
- Loss of income
- Loss of independence
- Loss of loved ones
- Loss of reputation

When losses invade this season of life, remember that negative thinking can produce negative feelings and can reveal a root of resentment. Rather than languishing among the losses, the Bible says ...

> **"Godliness with contentment
> is great gain."**
> **(1 Timothy 6:6)**

WHAT Causes Contribute to an Aversion to Aging?

As we age, our bodies change and our lives change, causing us to live in what can seem to be a state of constant transition. If we are not careful, these changes might derail what we know to be true. How important it is to cling to biblical truth to clarify our perspective and reestablish a correct mind-set.

Some of these challenging changes include:

ILLNESS

▶ As our body ages, we become more vulnerable to physical illness and injuries. Consequently, we need to prioritize keeping both our physical and spiritual lives healthy.

- **Natural Decline**

  "I'm getting older and my body doesn't work the same as it used to."

- **Biblical Reality**

  "The human spirit can endure in sickness, but a crushed spirit who can bear?" (Proverbs 18:14).

ISOLATION

▶ As family and friends begin to pass away, we can become isolated. Severe health issues can also cause isolation. Loneliness doesn't occur overnight, but over time, it can sap your strength and halt your hope.

- **Loneliness**

  "Since my spouse died and most of my friends aren't near, I feel so lonely."

- **Biblical Comfort**

  "Turn to me and be gracious to me, for I am lonely and afflicted" (Psalm 25:16).

DENIAL

▶ If you deny the truth about changes in your life, you cannot adapt to the change and embrace the growth that comes through maturity. Let go of the past and look forward to the future that God has planned for you.

- **Denial**

    "Age is just a number. I'm exactly the same person I've always been."

- **Biblical Certainty**

    "I focus on this one thing: Forgetting the past and looking forward to what lies ahead" (Philippians 3:13 NLT).

Fear

▶ If you hide "the real you" from others, it often becomes harder to develop safe and mature relationships based on honesty and trust. When you place your trust in God, He will drive away the fear and empower you to be "real" in all situations.

- **Fearfulness**

    "I'm afraid to ask for help with grocery shopping. They might think I can't go out alone or that I shouldn't be driving at all. I could lose my independence. I'm afraid I'll be rejected."

- **Biblical Truth**

    "There is no fear in love. But perfect love drives out fear" (1 John 4:18).

BITTERNESS

▶ Always wanting and expecting things to go *your way* leads to resentment against God and others when your expectations are not met. This leads to bitterness that hardens your heart, making it difficult to accept the unpredictability of life.

- **Bitterness**

  "I made many sacrifices while raising my children—now they ignore me."

- **Biblical Instruction**

  "See to it that no one falls short of the grace of God and that no bitter root grows up to cause trouble and defile many" (Hebrews 12:15).

PRIDE

▶ Placing your trust in your own efforts and believing you can be successful and content apart from God leads to an exaggerated sense of self-importance and blinds you to the truth of God's sovereignty.

- **Pridefulness**

  "God is never around when I need Him. I'm the only one who controls my future."

▪ Biblical Reminder

"In his pride the wicked man does not seek him; in all his thoughts there is no room for God" (Psalm 10:4).

REBELLION

▶ Disobedience toward God by seeking self-fulfillment in the false gods of greed, power, or immoral choices destroys commitment and the desire to serve the needs of others.

▪ Rebellion

"There's nothing wrong with getting a divorce if it means I have a chance for true love and happiness."

▪ Biblical Conviction

"'Only acknowledge your guilt—you have rebelled against the LORD your God ... and have not obeyed me,' declares the LORD" (Jeremiah 3:13).

Why do we worry about what we cannot change or control? When it comes to growing older, we fear the worst. We can't stop the hands of time, but we can take the good and make the best of everything else that aging has to offer. When we trust in the Lord, we will, one day, soar the heights on wings like eagles.

> **"Even youths grow tired and weary,**
> **and young men stumble and fall;**
> **but those who hope in the LORD**
> **will renew their strength.**
> **They will soar on wings like eagles;**
> **they will run and not grow weary,**
> **they will walk and not be faint."**
> **(Isaiah 40:30–31)**

Three God-Given Inner Needs

In reality, we have all been created with three God-given inner needs: the needs for love, significance, and security.[18]

▶ **Love**—to know that someone is unconditionally committed to our best interest

"My command is this: Love each other as I have loved you" (John 15:12).

▶ **Significance**—to know that our lives have meaning and purpose

"I cry out to God Most High, to God who fulfills his purpose for me" (Psalm 57:2 ESV).

▶ **Security**—to feel accepted and a sense of belonging

"Whoever fears the LORD has a secure fortress, and for their children it will be a refuge" (Proverbs 14:26).

Why did God give us these deep inner needs, knowing that people fail people and self-effort fails us as well?

God gave us these inner needs so that we would come to know Him as our Need-Meeter. Our needs are designed by God to draw us into a deeper dependence on Christ. God did not create any person or position or any amount of power or possessions to meet the deepest needs in our lives. If a person or thing *could* meet all our needs, we wouldn't need God! The Lord will use circumstances and bring positive people into our lives as an extension of His care and compassion, but ultimately only God can satisfy all the needs of our hearts. The Bible says …

**"The LORD will guide you always;
he will satisfy your needs
in a sun-scorched land
and will strengthen your frame.**

**You will be like a well-watered garden,
like a spring whose waters never fail."
(Isaiah 58:11)**

The apostle Paul revealed this truth by first asking, *"What a wretched man I am! Who will rescue me from this body that is subject to death?"* and then by answering his own question in saying it is *"Jesus Christ our Lord!"* (Romans 7:24–25).

All along, the Lord planned to meet our deepest needs for ...

▶ **Love**— *"I* [the Lord] *have loved you with an everlasting love; I have drawn you with unfailing kindness"* (Jeremiah 31:3).

▶ **Significance**— *"'For I know the plans I have for you,' declares the LORD, 'plans to prosper you and not to harm you, plans to give you hope and a future'"* (Jeremiah 29:11).

▶ **Security**— *"The LORD himself goes before you and will be with you; he will never leave you nor forsake you. Do not be afraid; do not be discouraged"* (Deuteronomy 31:8).

The truth is that our God-given needs for love, significance, and security can be legitimately met in Christ Jesus! Philippians 4:19 makes it plain: *"My God will meet all your needs according to the riches of his glory in Christ Jesus."*

▶ WRONG BELIEF

"There is no meaning left in life. I am useless, unloved, and a burden to others."

▶ RIGHT BELIEF

"Meaning and purpose for my life come from the indwelling presence of Christ, who is daily renewing my strength and growing His character in me."

**"We do not lose heart.
Though outwardly we are wasting away,
yet inwardly we are being renewed
day by day."
(2 Corinthians 4:16)**

WHAT Ageless Hope Does God Offer?

"This is the day that the LORD has made; let us rejoice and be glad in it" (Psalm 118:24 ESV).

Please note that this call to exultation has no exception clause! The word *"us"* refers to all people of all ages, living in anticipation of experiencing the God who has ordained each and every day. The winter years most certainly should provide ample moments for reflection, but they should also serve to acquire further opportunities for service to others and develop an ever deepening fellowship with God.

Can I Have a Meaningful Life with Eternal Security?

God intends for everyone to have a meaningful life, facing the future with an understanding of eternal security, resting in the full assurance that they will one day go to heaven based on the sacrificial provision for sin made available through His Son.

To enter into the fullness of God's plan, both now and for eternity, please heed the following *four* spiritual truths.

Four Points of God's Plan

1. God's Purpose for You is *Salvation*.

What was God's motivation in sending Jesus Christ to earth?

To express His love for you by saving you!

The Bible says, *"God so loved the world that he gave his one and only Son, that whoever believes in him shall not perish but have eternal life. For God did not send his Son into the world to condemn the world, but to save the world through him"* (John 3:16–17).

What was Jesus' purpose in coming to earth?

To forgive your sins, to empower you to have victory over sin, and to enable you to live a fulfilled life!

Jesus said, *"I have come that they may have life, and that they may have it more abundantly"* (John 10:10 NKJV).

2. Your Problem is *Sin*.

What exactly is sin?

Sin is living independently of God's standard—knowing what is right, but choosing what is wrong.

The Bible says, *"If anyone, then, knows the good they ought to do and doesn't do it, it is sin for them"* (James 4:17).

What is the major consequence of sin?

Spiritual death, eternal separation from God.

Scripture states, *"Your iniquities [sins] have separated you from your God"* (Isaiah 59:2).

"The wages of sin is death, but the gift of God is eternal life in Christ Jesus our Lord" (Romans 6:23).

3. God's Provision for You is the *Savior*.

Can anything remove the penalty for sin?

Yes! Jesus died on the cross to personally pay the penalty for your sins.

The Bible says, *"God demonstrates his own love for us in this: While we were still sinners, Christ died for us"* (Romans 5:8).

What is the solution to being separated from God?

Belief in (entrusting your life to) Jesus Christ as the only way to God the Father.

Jesus says, *"I am the way and the truth and the life. No one comes to the Father except through me"* (John 14:6).

"Believe in the Lord Jesus, and you will be saved" (Acts 16:31).

4. Your Part is *Surrender.*

Give Christ control of your life, entrusting yourself to Him.

"Jesus said to his disciples, 'Whoever wants to be my disciple must deny themselves and take up their cross [die to your own self-rule] and follow me. For whoever wants to save their life will lose it, but whoever loses their life for me will find it. What good will it be for someone to gain the whole world, yet forfeit their soul?'" (Matthew 16:24–26).

Place your faith in (rely on) Jesus Christ as your personal Lord and Savior and reject your "good works" as a means of earning God's approval.

"It is by grace you have been saved, through faith—and this is not from yourselves, it is the gift of God—not by works, so that no one can boast" (Ephesians 2:8–9).

The moment you choose to receive Jesus as your Lord and Savior—entrusting your life to Him—He comes to live inside you. Then He gives you His power to live the fulfilled life God has planned for you. If you want to be fully forgiven by God and become the person God created you to be, you can tell Him in a simple, heartfelt prayer like this:

PRAYER OF SALVATION

"God, I want a real relationship with You.
I admit that many times
I've chosen to go my own way
instead of Your way.
Please forgive me for my sins.
Jesus, thank You for dying on the cross
to pay the penalty for my sins.
Come into my life to be my Lord
and my Savior.
Change me from the inside out
and make me the person
You created me to be.
In Your holy name I pray. Amen."

What Can You Now Expect?

If you sincerely prayed this prayer, look at what God says about you!

**"Very truly I tell you,
whoever hears my word
and believes him who sent me has
eternal life and will not be judged
but has crossed over from death to life."
(John 5:24)**

STEPS TO SOLUTION

The youngest sibling in the Ray family is Ruth. In her 70s and early 80s she shared her wise insights in HOPE FOR THE HEART's *Ministry Magazine*. In one of her regular "Granny Ruth's Recipes for Living" columns, she highlighted the topic of aging as seen here:

RAYS OF SUNSHINE FROM RUTH RAY HUNT

Growing old has its advantages. You glance through a magazine and already know that the face cream will not miraculously make you twenty again! You know that the friends you've had through the years recognize the many facets of your personality and still love you! You can be a child again with your grandchildren, smile at everyone at the supermarket without being considered "bold," and if the mood hits, you know that a little eccentricity can be fascinating!

Your treasures are your family and friends, and close behind are books—with large print. You relate to the pain of others so well because you have experienced so much yourself, and you remember that without pain you would never really know the true meaning of joy.

Most reassuring is the fact that God still has a purpose for you. A lifetime of love and laughter—losses and learning—has given you the wisdom He intends for you to share with others.

Growing older has more advantages. Of course, you don't look the same (and you never, ever look into the mirror), but somehow your face has character! You stop worrying about your shape and are thankful your legs still carry you upstairs at night. Now life falls more accurately into perspective. Major issues still remain important, but what was once an irritation is now irrelevant.

You learn to compensate for nature's toll with spare glasses in every room. You realize that without them, you could never find anything—least of all the ones you need to help you see! You begin to see those dreadful hearing aids as a blessing in disguise—for peace and quiet are yours whenever you want it!

Sometimes you may even be privileged to pass on your "secret." The secret that helped you through it all—that God is your Rock, always there for you when the road is rough, always surrounding you with love when there's no one else. So grow old and delight in it—that way your heart will be forever young! The Bible says, *"He will renew your life and sustain you in your old age"* (Ruth 4:15).

Nine Lessons Learned "From My Rearview Mirror"

There are so many lessons I've learned as I've aged—lessons I never knew when I was young:

- ▶ I've learned that every day we should reach out and touch someone. People love human touch—holding hands, warm hugs, or just friendly pats on the back.

- ▶ I've learned that making a living is not the same as making a life.

- ▶ I've learned that the Lord likes giving second chances.

- ▶ I've learned that if you pursue happiness, it will elude you. But if you focus on the needs of others, happiness will find you.

- ▶ I've learned that whenever I decide to do something kind, I make the right decision.

- ▶ I've learned that even when I have pain, I don't have to be one.

- ▶ I've learned that no matter what I know, I still have a lot to learn.

- ▶ I've learned that everyone needs a little something just to make them smile.

- ▶ I've learned that everyone on earth needs prayer. And praying is something I can always do.

Key Verse to Memorize

Looking in the mirror, you may be reminded of how much you have changed since your younger days. And when reviewing your life, it may appear that nothing has remained constant or predictable. Nevertheless, one thing remains unchanged—God's unconditional, unquenchable love and abiding presence in your life. The One who formed you in your mother's womb has walked alongside you every day of your life— even in times when you felt lost and alone—even when you mentally, emotionally, or spiritually distanced yourself from Him.

As we experience God's faithfulness in many different ways—sustaining us, carrying us, rescuing us—His Word assures us that when our bodies become weak, we can rely on His sustaining strength to help us each and every day.

> *"Even to your old age*
> *and gray hairs I am he,*
> *I am he who will sustain you.*
> *I have made you and I will carry you;*
> *I will sustain you and I will rescue you."*
> (Isaiah 46:4)

Key Passage to Read

What is God's perspective regarding our purpose *here* and our ultimate destination *there*? Paul addresses this question by urging us to look beyond our *momentary* problems here on earth and focus on our heavenly future. When God calls us home, we will trade our frail bodies (described as *"tents"*) for *"a building from God, an eternal house in heaven"* (2 Corinthians 5:1). Meditate on this passage and take comfort in God's divine assurance of your eternal life with the Creator and Shepherd of your soul.

2 Corinthians 4:17–5:10

17"For our light and momentary troubles are achieving for us an eternal glory that far outweighs them all.

18So we fix our eyes not on what is seen, but on what is unseen, since what is seen is temporary, but what is unseen is eternal.

5:1For we know that if the earthly tent we live in is destroyed, we have a building from God, an eternal house in heaven, not built by human hands.

2Meanwhile we groan, longing to be clothed instead with our heavenly dwelling,

3because when we are clothed, we will not be found naked.

⁴For while we are in this tent, we groan and are burdened, because we do not wish to be unclothed but to be clothed instead with our heavenly dwelling, so that what is mortal may be swallowed up by life.

⁵Now the one who has fashioned us for this very purpose is God, who has given us the Spirit as a deposit, guaranteeing what is to come.

⁶Therefore we are always confident and know that as long as we are at home in the body we are away from the Lord.

⁷For we live by faith, not by sight.

⁸We are confident, I say, and would prefer to be away from the body and at home with the Lord.

⁹So we make it our goal to please him, whether we are at home in the body or away from it.

¹⁰For we must all appear before the judgment seat of Christ, that each of us may receive what is due us for the things done while in the body, whether good or bad."

An Eternal Perspective

▶ "I will **view** life's trials as opportunities for gaining eternal glory." (v. 4:17)

▶ "I will **set** my mind on the unseen, which is eternal." (v. 4:18)

▶ "I will **realize** that what I see is merely temporary." (v. 4:18)

▶ "I will **know** that when my earthly body dies, God will give me an eternal body." (v. 5:1)

▶ "I will **regard** longing for eternity as normal because I'll then be clothed with immortality." (vv. 5:2–3)

▶ "I will **acknowledge** that this life will always have hardship, loss, and grief." (v. 5:4)

▶ "I will **accept** that aging is part of God's marvelous plan for my life." (v. 5:5)

▶ "I will **depend** on God's gift of the Holy Spirit within me as my source of strength." (v. 5:5)

▶ "I will **see** life through the eyes of faith." (v. 5:7)

▶ "I will **look** forward to my eternal home with the Lord." (v. 5:8)

▶ "I will **make** it my goal to please God." (v. 5:9)

▶ "I will **appear** before the judgment seat of Christ." (v. 5:10)

MY Personalized Plan

The purpose of developing a personalized plan is to take stock of your life, inquire of God, listen to Him, and learn from Him—from His Word, from the promptings of His Spirit, from circumstances, and from the godly people He places in your life to speak His truth. It is the cry of the psalmist that resonates within the hearts of all who have finished the first seasons of life and are moving on to the latter ones.

"Search me, God,
and know my heart;
test me and know my anxious thoughts.
See if there is any offensive way in me,
and lead me in the way everlasting."
(Psalm 139:23–24)

An Acrostic for AGING

At this point in your life, as you look back at who you once were and who you are now—at what God has accomplished in and through you—and as you contemplate how it would please God for you to spend the remaining part of your life, plan to prayerfully ...

A ccentuate the positive.

There are times when you may feel overwhelmed with negative emotions and utterly discouraged about your life. It's during these times you can relate to David's lament: *"My soul is downcast within me"* (Psalm 42:6). It is also during these times you need to take charge of your mind-set and attitudes.

▶ Realize, your feelings are usually determined by your thinking—by what you choose to think about and dwell on. Guard your thoughts.

▶ Remember that God is working for your good in all circumstances, and He will use every situation in your life to conform you more and more into the likeness of His Son.

▶ Practice God's instruction to give thanks. Praise Him in all things, realizing He is sovereign over all the earth and all that happens within it and within your life as well.

▶ Look for the good in people and in circumstances, asking God to reveal His good purposes for you.

▶ Choose to align your thinking with God's Word, taking each thought captive and passing it through God's grid concerning what you think, say, and do.

"Whatever is true, whatever is noble, whatever is right, whatever is pure, whatever is lovely, whatever is admirable—if anything is excellent or praiseworthy—think about such things" (Philippians 4:8).

G et on the highway to health.

"Old habits die hard," but good health often depends on developing new habits that reduce the risks for serious and disabling health problems, such as heart disease, stroke, diabetes, cancer, osteoporosis, and obesity. God calls us to be good stewards of the gifts He has given us—including our health.

▶ Sleep at least seven to eight consecutive hours.

▶ Maintain a healthy weight. Eat a healthy, high-fiber breakfast each morning and a variety of nutritious foods, including plenty of fruits, vegetables, whole grains, and low-fat dairy products throughout the day. Avoid sugary foods and saturated and trans fats. Always check with your doctor before changing your diet.

▶ Get regular medical checkups and recommended disease screenings to detect health problems early, when they are most easily treated.

▶ Exercise regularly, aiming for at least 30 minutes of physical activity every day. Walking, peddling a stationary bike, swimming, water aerobics, and playing Ping-Pong are beneficial ways to keep fit. Check with your doctor before starting an exercise program.

▶ Engage in exercises that stimulate your brain, such as reading about people and places unfamiliar to you, learning a new skill, or working crossword puzzles.

"Dear friend, I pray that you may enjoy good health and that all may go well with you, even as your soul is getting along well" (3 John 2).

I nitiate involvement.

God's purpose is for you to be involved in the lives of others in positive and constructive ways. The world is full of people who are lonely and in need of the encouragement and companionship of someone who sincerely cares. Being attentive to the needs of others will automatically take the focus off your own problems—and will help you put your own difficulties into perspective.

▶ Visit the homebound or those who are otherwise confined.

▶ Learn to listen with care and compassion.

▶ Volunteer your time and assistance with an organization or cause you believe in.

▶ Encourage others by talking to them. Ask questions that draw them out in conversation.

▶ Form a neighborhood, weekly Bible study group.

"Whoever sows generously will also reap generously" (2 Corinthians 9:6).

Notice the roses.

Give yourself permission to "slow down and smell the roses." Overextending yourself leads to *stress*, which over time, can rob you of energy and joy. Find a balance between being busy and taking a breather. Make time to be still and listen for God's voice.

- ▶ Limit your commitments to what feels manageable.
- ▶ Take time to identify and renew previous interests. Learn to relax and play.
- ▶ Visit local museums, galleries, and other places of interest.
- ▶ Set aside time for taking leisurely strolls around town or drives in the countryside.
- ▶ Gain appreciation for the beauty in nature.

"When I look at your heavens, the work of your fingers, the moon and the stars, which you have set in place, what is man that you are mindful of him, and the son of man that you care for him?" (Psalm 8:3–4 ESV).

Grow in grace.

God invites you to draw near to Him through each season of your life. His desire is for you to have a loving, personal relationship with Him through His Son, Jesus Christ. Growing in grace simply means that you are becoming more like Christ. As you become increasingly aware of His presence, you are becoming less attached to the things of this world. Loving others becomes easier, and your conflict with the will of God lessens. The losses you face as you move through the aging process become the natural bridge to a deeper dependence on God.

▶ Read a Christian devotional in the morning and at bedtime.

▶ Join a weekly Bible study led by Christian leaders at your church or in the community.

▶ Appreciate how God has shown His love throughout your life.

▶ Listen to what God is saying to your heart.

▶ Meditate on the goodness and greatness of God.

"Grow in the grace and knowledge of our Lord and Savior Jesus Christ. To him be glory both now and forever!" (2 Peter 3:18).

HOW TO Overcome Loneliness

Loneliness is common to everyone, yet it can be controlled. Consider carefully examining the elements of loneliness in your own life. Knowledge alone cannot solve the problems caused by loneliness, but knowledge coupled with wisdom can be helpful in limiting the negative effects of loneliness in your life. While loneliness feels like an emotional problem based on unchangeable circumstances, it is actually a perception problem that can lead to emotional problems.

BRANCH OUT FROM LONELINESS BY REACHING OUT TO FRIENDS

When you experience a season of loneliness, reach out to …

▶ **CASUAL FRIENDS** with whom you have:

- Occasional contact but common interests and activities

- Some knowledge of accomplishments, abilities, and character qualities

- Concern for personal problems

"I hope to see you soon, and we will talk face to face. Peace to you. The friends here send their greetings. Greet the friends there by name" (3 John 14).

▶ **CLOSE FRIENDS** with whom you have:

- Regular contact and mutual interests and activities

- Sensitivity to likes, dislikes, strengths, and weaknesses

- Shared God's comfort during trials and sorrows

"Do two walk together unless they have agreed to do so?" (Amos 3:3).

▶**COMMITTED FRIENDS** with whom you have:

- Scheduled time together and shared values, goals, experiences, and commitments

- Freedom to help correct character flaws

- Personal involvement in defending a reputation

"Where you go I will go, and where you stay I will stay" (Ruth 1:16–17).

HOW TO Walk in Wisdom

The way we view our circumstances shapes our outlook on life. You can view winter as a cold, dreary, lifeless season—or feel peaceful in the tranquility and restfulness it represents in God's design. God calls us to view our "winter years" with hope and acceptance, seeing this time of life with new eyes. What lessons can this season teach us?

"Age should speak; advanced years should teach wisdom."
(Job 32:7)

▶ **Winter is the season of splendor.**

- As you treasure the memories of the past and look for the splendor of life in the present, you live for the glory of Christ in the future.

  "The glory of young men is their strength, gray hair the splendor of the old" (Proverbs 20:29).

▶ **Winter's storehouse holds a wealth of wisdom.**

- You have a greater understanding of God's truths, and you base your daily decisions on God's Word.

  "Whoever heeds life-giving correction will be at home among the wise" (Proverbs 15:31).

▶ **Winter thrives on its deeper roots.**

- You love on a deeper level, and your relationships become more precious and meaningful.

  "They will be like a tree planted by the water that sends out its roots by the stream. It does not fear when heat comes; its leaves are always green. It has no worries in a year of drought and never fails to bear fruit" (Jeremiah 17:8).

▶ **Winter accepts its own barrenness.**

- You see yourself as you are today, with no longing for what used to be. This gives you the freedom to accept yourself and to be yourself.

"There is now no condemnation for those who are in Christ Jesus" (Romans 8:1).

▶ Winter opens the door to new life.

- You are an example to others of how to live a godly life, as you reflect His light and love into the world.

"In everything set them an example by doing what is good. In your teaching show integrity, seriousness and soundness of speech that cannot be condemned, so that those who oppose you may be ashamed because they have nothing bad to say about us" (Titus 2:7–8).

▶ Winter has no fear of death.

- You are more optimistic and more peaceful, trusting in the goodness of God's plan for your life.

"No eye has seen, no ear has heard, and no mind has imagined what God has prepared for those who love him." (1 Corinthians 2:9 NLT).

▶ Winter knows it is here for only a season.

- You loosen your hold on the things of this world, understanding the difference between what brings fleeting happiness and what provides lasting peace and joy.

"Our citizenship is in heaven. And we eagerly await a Savior from there, the Lord Jesus Christ" (Philippians 3:20).

▶ **Winter hears the call to eternal life.**

- You rest in the relationship with the Shepherd of your soul, who promises you eternal life.

  "My sheep listen to my voice; I know them, and they follow me. I give them eternal life, and they shall never perish; no one will snatch them out of my hand" (John 10:27–28).

▶ **Winter rests in its hope for the future.**

- You no longer fear death, but are grateful for each day of life, and peacefully accept that the Lord will call you home one victorious day.

  "Where, O death, is your victory? Where, O death, is your sting?" (1 Corinthians 15:55).

When the beauty and strength of spring is gone, it is sometimes difficult to accept the losses that come with life's passing seasons. But all changes—even the unwanted and unexpected ones—bring opportunities for growth and new beginnings.

The most common crime of the 21st century doesn't involve gun violence, hijacking, or kidnapping. No, the crimes considered "low-risk"—the ones most unreported—are financial scams against seniors. Why are seniors such a suitable target? Because crooks think older folks have lots of money sitting in their accounts just waiting to be plundered. But not only are wealthy seniors being robbed, low-income seniors are at risk as well.[19]

EIGHT WAYS TO PROTECT YOURSELF AGAINST SCAMS[20]

Millions of older adults fall victim to scams every year. We all need to know how to protect ourselves and our older loved ones from scam artists—especially those who target the elderly.

1. You are at risk not only from strangers, but also from those close to you.

- Sadly, over 90% of all reported elder abuse is committed by a senior's own family members. Therefore, you must learn who you can and cannot trust. Those who most often prey on older adults are their own adult children, followed by grandchildren, nieces and nephews, and others.

- Everyone is at risk of financial abuse, even those without substantial income or assets. Learn about common scams.

2. Don't isolate—stay active and involved!

- Being isolated increases your risks for "elder abuse." Family violence usually occurs behind closed doors, and *elder abuse* is no different.

- Get involved in your local church and visit a local senior center to meet new people and find new activities.

3. Door-to-door salespeople and phone solicitors are not "your new friends."

- You are not obligated to purchase anything just because someone comes to your home or calls you on the phone. Make it a practice to say: "I never buy from (or give to) anyone who visits or calls unannounced." If the solicitor asks for personal information say, "I don't give out that information. Goodbye." Then close the door or hang up the phone.

- Never make a donation or purchase that requires you to write your credit card information on a form. Use cash or write a check if you know the person, such as a neighbor child selling cookies for a fundraiser.

4. Take care with your credit card receipts.

- Identity theft is a huge racket. To protect yourself, use a paper shredder to shred receipts you don't need to keep.

- Always monitor your monthly credit card statements. Mark through all but the last four digits of your credit card number on other receipts you need to keep for warranty purposes.

5. Protect your mail and monitor your credit reports annually.

- Don't leave incoming mail in your mailbox for long periods of time. When sending sensitive mail, consider taking it directly to the post office or dropping it in a secure collection box.

- Regularly monitor your credit ratings and watch for unusual or incorrect information. In the U.S., you can obtain a free report once every 12 months from each of the three credit reporting agencies through www.annualcreditreport.com.

6. Use your bank's direct deposit and bill pay services.

- Using direct deposit ensures that benefit and pension checks go straight into your account and are protected.

- Clever scammers and even unscrupulous loved ones have stolen checks from mailboxes or seniors' homes when left out in the open.

7. **Never give out your credit card, banking, or other personal information over the phone unless you initiate the call.**

- These groups already have your information and they won't call you looking for such information. They would understand if you choose to call them directly to verify.

- Insurance and Medicare fraud is one of the largest scams involving seniors. Common schemes include billing for services never delivered and selling unneeded devices or services to beneficiaries.

- Protect giving out these identification numbers and don't allow anyone else to use them. Be wary of salespeople who try to sell you something they claim will be completely paid for by insurance or Medicare.

8. **Don't be "people-pressured"—do your research.**

- Become informed and "shop around" before you buy. Take a friend who can offer wise counsel concerning difficult decisions.

- Carefully read all contracts and purchasing agreements before you sign. Make certain that all you require and have agreed to has been put in writing. Understand all the contract cancellation and refund terms. Don't be pressured into making purchases, signing contracts, or committing funds. Consider asking someone you trust to accompany you to confirm your understanding of all the details. But remember, these decisions are ultimately yours and yours alone.

Elder Abuse

QUESTION: "What is elder abuse, and what can I do if I suspect abuse?"

ANSWER: Elder abuse is any intentional or negligent act that causes harm or loss to an older person. Most cases of elder abuse go undetected and thus unreported, leaving the elderly feeling devalued, dejected, and demoralized. Acts that constitute abuse include:

- Abandonment

- Exploitation

- Emotional or psychological mistreatment

- Neglect

- Financial abuse

- Physical abuse

- Sexual abuse

- Verbal Abuse

Abuse has only to be suspected, not proven, by the person reporting it. Professionals investigating the report are the ones responsible for verifying the legitimacy of the report.

To report suspected elder abuse in the community, contact the local *Adult Protective Services* or *Eldercare Locator*. To report suspected abuse in a nursing home or long-term care facility, contact your local *Long-Term Care Ombudsman*.

The *National Center on Elder Abuse* helps communities, agencies, and organizations ensure that elders and adults with disabilities can live with dignity, without experiencing abuse, neglect, and exploitation. It provides education, research, and helpful suggestions for stopping abuse.

The Bible says ...

**"Speak up for those
who cannot speak for themselves."
(Proverbs 31:8)**

SCRIPTURES TO MEMORIZE

Who can **still bear fruit in old age**?

> *"The righteous will flourish like a palm tree ... They will **still bear fruit in old age**."* (Psalm 92:12, 14)

In time of need, why do we need to **approach God's throne of grace with confidence**?

> *"Let us then **approach God's throne of grace with confidence**, so that we may receive mercy and find grace to help us **in** our **time of need**"* (Hebrews 4:16).

What happens when my body, my "**earthly tent,**" **is destroyed**?

> *"For we know that if the **earthly tent** we live in **is destroyed**, we have a building from God, an eternal house in heaven"* (2 Corinthians 5:1).

What should my **advanced years** produce?

> *"I thought, 'Age should speak; **advanced years** should teach wisdom' "* (Job 32:7).

Can I rely on the promises of God to **carry** me, **sustain** me, and **rescue** me?

> *"Even to your old age and gray hairs ... I will **carry** you; I will **sustain** you and I will **rescue** you"* (Isaiah 46:4).

NOTES

1. Henri-Federic Amiel, in *The Westminser Collection of Christian Quotations*, ed. by Martin H. Manser, (Louisville, KY: Westminster John Knox Press, 2001), 263.

2. James Strong, *Strong's Hebrew Lexicon*, electronic edition; Online Bible Millennium Edition v. 1.13, (Timnathserah Inc., July 6, 2002).

3. *Merriam-Webster's Collegiate Dictionary*, electronic ed. (n.p.: Merriam-Webster, 2001), s.v. "gerontology," http://www.merriam-webster.com/dictionary/gerontology.

4. *World Health Organization*, "World Health Statistics 2014," News Release, May 14, 2014, http://www.who.int/mediacentre/news/releases/2014/world-health-statistics-2014/en/.

5. *Disabled World*, "How Long Will I Live—Life Expectancy Chart," Ian Langtree, revised November 10, 2015, http://www.disabled-world.com/calculators-charts/life-expectancy-statistics.php.

6. For this section see *Our World in Data*, "Life Expectancy," (2015) Max Roser, accessed December 2, 2015, http://ourworldindata.org/data/population-growth-vital-statistics/life-expectancy/.

7. For this section see *Social Security*, "Calculators: Life Expectancy," accessed November 30, 2015, https://www.ssa.gov/planners/lifeexpectancy.html.

8. *Merck Manual, Consumer Version*, "Overview of Aging," by Richard W. Besdine, MD, accessed November 30, 2015, http://www.merckmanuals.com/home/older-people-s-health-issues/the-aging-body/overview-of-aging.

9. *Better Health Channel*, "Healthy Ageing—Staying Mentally Active," accessed November 30, 2015, https://www.betterhealth.vic.gov.au/health/healthyliving/healthy-ageing-stay-mentally-active.

10. *Association for Psychological Science*, Observer, "The Golden Years of Emotion: Lifespan Research," by Susanne Schiebe, accessed December 1, 2015, https://www.psychologicalscience.org/observer/the-golden-years-of-emotion

11. *LifeHope&Truth*, "Dealing With Aging," by Mary Clark, accessed December 1, 2015, http://lifehopeandtruth.com/relationships/aging/dealing-with-aging/.

12. June Hunt, *Midlife Crisis: Facing the Fork in the Road*, Biblical Counseling Keys Library, (Dallas: Hope For The Heart, 2008), 1.

13. Joshua Kendall, *The Man Who Made Lists* (New York: G. P. Putnam's Sons, 2008); *Time Rime*, "Peter Roget, Persistance of Vision," accessed December 9, 2015, http://timerime.com/en/event/1224454/Peter+Roget+Persistence+of+vision/; Barbara Walraff, "Organization Man," in *The Wilson Quarterly*, Spring 2008, accessed December 9, 2015, https://wilsonquarterly.com/quarterly/spring-2008-backbone-infrastructure-for-americas-future/organization-man/; *BBC History*, "Peter Mark Roget," accessed December 9, 2015, http://www.bbc.co.uk/history/historic_figures/roget_peter_mark.shtml.

14. Frank Minirth, John Reed, and Paul Meier, *Beating the Clock: A Guide for Maturing Successfully* (Richardson, TX: Today, 1985), 39–40.

15. *American Psychological Society*, "Older Adults Health and Age-Related Changes," accessed December 3, 2015, http://www.apa.org/pi/aging/resources/guides/older.aspx.

16. J. D. Carter, "Maturity," in *Wholeness and Holiness: Readings in the Psychology/Theology of Mental Health*, ed. H. N. Malony (Grand Rapids: Baker, 1983), 184–190, as cited in Raymond T. Brock, "Ministering to the Aging," in *The Holy Spirit and Counseling: Principles and Practice*, ed. Marvin G. Gilbert and Raymond T. Brock (Peabody, MA: Hendrickson, 1988), 131.

17. George Congreve, *Christian Life: A Response with Other Retreat Addresses and Sermons* (London: Longmans, Green, and Co., 1899), 164.

18. Lawrence J. Crabb, Jr., *Understanding People: Deep Longings for Relationship*, Ministry Resources Library (Grand Rapids: Zondervan, 1987), 15–16; Robert S. McGee, *The Search for Significance*, 2nd ed. (Houston, TX: Rapha, 1990), 27–30.

19. *National Council on Aging* (ncoa), "Top 10 Financial Scams Tarketing Seniors," accessed December 10, 2015, https://www.ncoa.org/economic-security/ money-management/scams-security/top-10-scams- targeting-seniors/?print=t.

20. This section adapted from *National Council on Aging* (ncoa), "How Seniors Can Protect Themselves Against Money Scams," accessed December 10, 2015, https://www.ncoa.org/economic-security/money- management/scams-security/protection-from-scams/.

HOPE FOR THE HEART TITLES

- *Adultery*
- *Aging Well*
- *Alcohol & Drug Abuse*
- *Anger*
- *Anorexia & Bulimia*
- *Boundaries*
- *Bullying*
- *Caregiving*
- *Chronic Illness & Disability*
- *Codependency*
- *Conflict Resolution*
- *Confrontation*
- *Considering Marriage*
- *Critical Spirit*
- *Decision Making*
- *Depression*
- *Domestic Violence*
- *Dysfunctional Family*
- *Envy & Jealousy*
- *Fear*
- *Financial Freedom*
- *Forgiveness*
- *Friendship*
- *Gambling*
- *Grief*
- *Guilt*
- *Hope*
- *Loneliness*
- *Manipulation*
- *Marriage*
- *Overeating*
- *Parenting*
- *Perfectionism*
- *Procrastination*
- *Reconciliation*
- *Rejection*
- *Self-Worth*
- *Sexual Integrity*
- *Singleness*
- *Spiritual Abuse*
- *Stress*
- *Success Through Failure*
- *Suicide Prevention*
- *Trials*
- *Verbal & Emotional Abuse*
- *Victimization*

www.aspirepress.com